E F r H H ε N o p a V X W Z y Z

a Christmas gift for:

_____

from:

_____

CHRISTMAS

fun facts for kids

A to Z

Editorial Director: Todd Hafer
Art Director: Kevin Swanson
Designer: Michelle Nicolier
Production Artist: Dan Horton

Manuscript written and prepared
by Scott Degelman and Associates.

ISBN 978-1-59530-159-8
BOK6070
Printed and bound in China.

CHRISTMAS

fun facts for kids

A to Z

GIFT BOOKS
from Hallmark

Introduction

If you're reading this book, chances are that Christmas is coming soon! During the Christmas season, people around the world remember Jesus' miraculous birth in a stable in Bethlehem more than 2,000 years ago.

As you journey from A to Z, you'll explore some of the mysteries and unusual circumstances surrounding the Savior's birth—and how it's celebrated. And we hope you'll love and respect Jesus more than ever. So let's learn more about Christmas—it's fun, and it's as easy as A, B, C.

a

is for Advent

The 24 days before Christmas are called Advent. The Advent season begins on the fourth Sunday before Christmas and ends on Christmas Eve. During Advent, people around the world remember and celebrate how Jesus came to earth more than 2,000 years ago. They think about what Jesus' birth meant to those who lived long ago—and what it means to us today.

This book can be your companion this Christmas season. If you want to read the book as part of your Advent activities, just begin on December 1 and read a page a day. You'll finish on Christmas Eve, the last day of Advent.

b

is for Bethlehem

Jesus wasn't the only famous person born in Bethlehem. David, the great king (and giant-slayer), was born there, too. And did you know that 700 years before Jesus' birth, a prophet named Micah predicted the Savior would be born in Bethlehem (Micah 5:2)?

C
is for Candles

Jesus once told his followers, "I am the light of the world" (John 8:12). To help them remember this message, Christians of long ago began displaying candles at Christmastime. As you see all the candles and lights this year, let them remind you that Jesus' words and actions are our light. They show us how we should live.

d

is for Dream

Have you ever dreamed about angels? That's what happened to Joseph, Jesus' earthly father (Matthew 1:18-25). Joseph was engaged to Mary, Jesus' mother, but then he began to have second thoughts about marrying her. That's when an angel visited Joseph's dreams one night. "Don't be afraid to take Mary as your wife," the angel told him. Joseph obeyed. After all, who would want to disobey an angel?

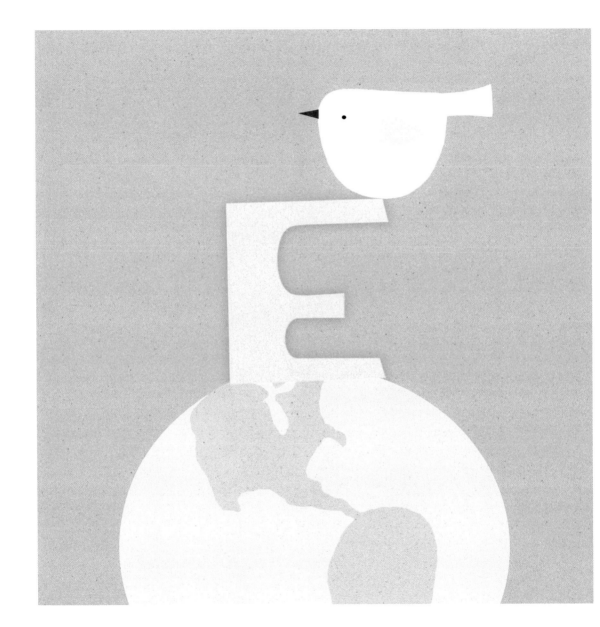

e

is for Earth

The Bible tells us that the heavens, where God lives, are much higher than the earth (Isaiah 55:9). When Jesus came down to earth as a tiny baby, he left behind his wonderful home in heaven. But he loved us so much that he was willing to come such a long way.

f

is for Francis of Assisi

You've probably seen many manger scenes this Christmas season—little models of Jesus, Mary, Joseph, and the shepherds and wise men. Perhaps you've also enjoyed a "living nativity," with people playing various parts—along with real animals.

The man who "invented" the manger scene was Saint Francis of Assisi. Way back in 1224, Saint Francis decided that he wanted to re-create the night Jesus was born. So he built a stable and dressed people as Mary, Joseph, and the shepherds. He used a wax doll to represent the baby Jesus. He even put a real donkey, some cows, and some sheep in his stable. Saint Francis hoped his manger scene would help people remember God's gift of his son.

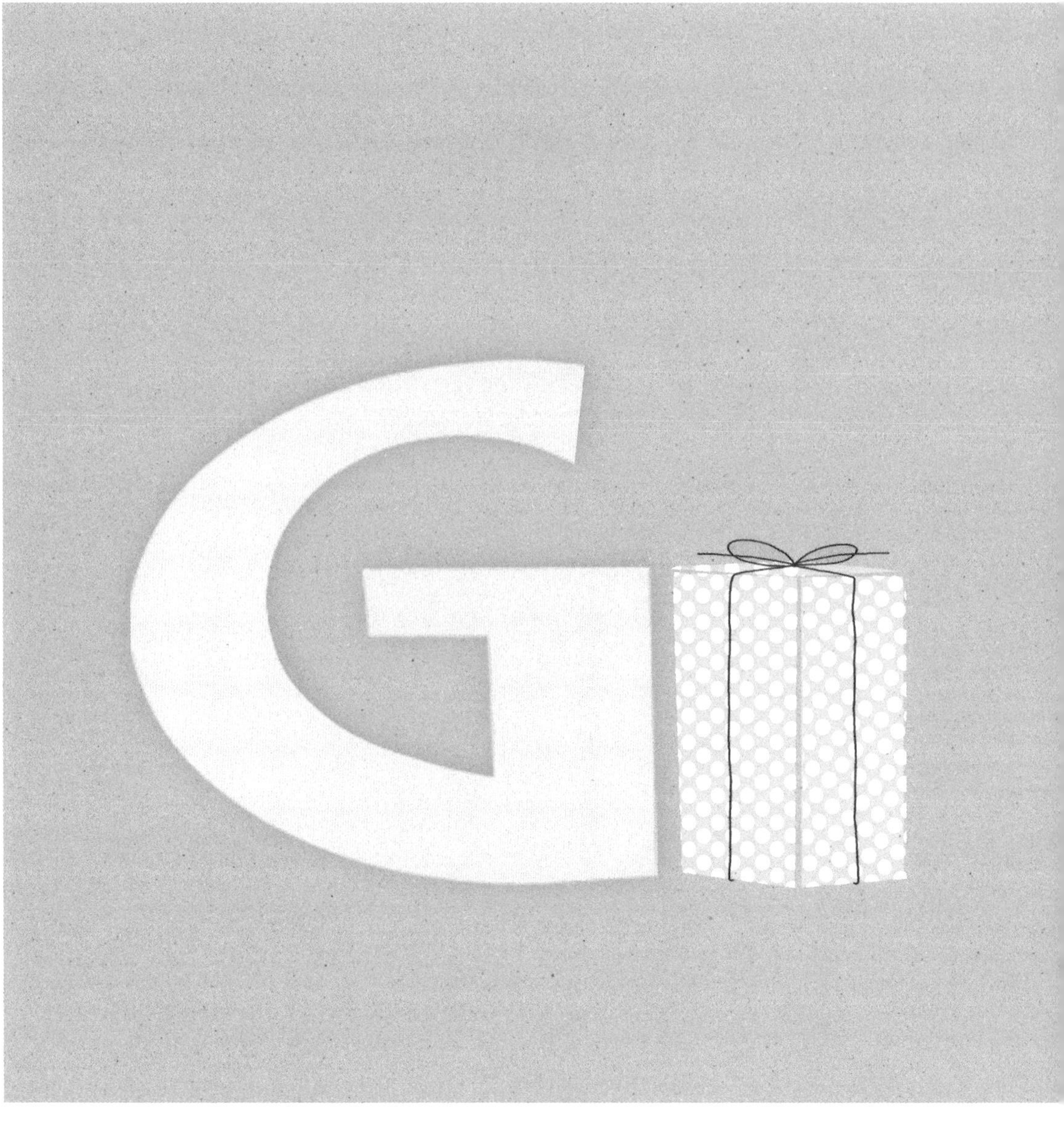
G

g

is for Gifts

What gifts do you hope you'll get this Christmas? People have been giving each other gifts for thousands of years, but gift giving and Christmas have a special connection because the Magi (or wise men) brought presents of gold, frankincense, and myrrh to the baby Jesus.

Can you think of a present you could give Jesus this Christmas? Like being extra kind to your family? Or donating something to someone who needs it more? Remember, Jesus taught us that when we help someone less fortunate than we are, it's just like we are helping him (Matthew 25:40)!

h

is for Heavenly Hosts

The night Jesus was born, some shepherds got to hear a heavenly concert (Luke 2:8-15). A whole host of angels appeared to them, singing a song of praise to Jesus. Singing is one way we can show love and honor to the Lord—even if we can't hit high notes like an angel!

i

is for Infant

When an infant is born, it weighs only seven pounds or so (about as much as a house cat) and is completely helpless. A baby needs parents for protection and food. Jesus chose to come down to earth as a tiny baby so that he could grow up and experience what it's like to be human. When you pray to Jesus, remember that you're talking to someone who knows how you feel.

j

is for Jesus

Before the Lord was born, the angel Gabriel told Mary to name her child Jesus (Luke 1:31). The name Jesus means "the Lord saves." By the way, Jesus is also the Greek word for Joshua, the guy who marched around Jericho.

k

is for King Herod

Not everyone was excited about Jesus' birth. Herod, the wicked king of Jerusalem, which is near Bethlehem, was jealous when he heard of another king being born. He tried to trick the wise men (whom you'll read more about later) into telling him where the baby Jesus was. Herod planned to kill Jesus once he found him. However, the wise men were warned in a dream not to tell Herod anything, so they snuck back to their home country without revealing anything.

Then an angel appeared to Joseph again and told him to take Mary and baby Jesus and flee to a faraway land called Egypt. The family waited in Egypt until Herod died and it was safe to return home (Matthew 2:1-21).

L

is for Love

More than anything else, the Christmas season is about love. Joseph and Mary loved each other and they loved the baby Jesus. And God loves all of us so much that he sent his son to be the first and greatest Christmas gift of all. Jesus is a gift from God, with love (John 3:16).

m

is for Mary

Imagine being Jesus' mother. Now that's a huge responsibility! But Mary was brave and eager to serve God any way she could. When the angel Gabriel told her that she would give birth to the Son of God, she said, "I am the Lord's servant. May it be to me as you have said" (Luke 1:38).

n

is for Noel

Have you seen, heard, and sung the word "Noel" a lot this holiday season? "Noel" is how people say "Christmas" in France. The word comes from shortening the French phrase *les bonnes nouvelles,* which means "the good news"—the good news that Jesus came to earth to teach, to heal the sick, and, most important, to show his power over sin and death.

O

is for Ornaments

Martin Luther, a German preacher who lived about 500 years ago, is credited with inventing the custom of bringing a Christmas tree into a home, then decorating it with shiny, shimmering ornaments and tinsel.

One Christmas Eve, Martin was strolling in the woods, admiring the tall fir trees standing against a starry sky. He cut down one of the trees, carried it home, and decorated it with candles. (Let's hope he was careful!) Then he gathered his children around the twinkling candles and told them how they reminded him of the stars that shone above Bethlehem the night Jesus was born.

p

is for Promise

When Jesus came to earth, it was one way God kept a promise to his people. For many years, preachers like Micah (remember him?) had told people that a Messiah would arrive on the scene and help them solve their problems. Isaiah, writing 700 years before Christ's birth, revealed this promise about the Messiah: "For to us a child is born, to us a son is given, and the government will be on his shoulders. And he will be called Wonderful Counselor, Mighty God, Everlasting Father, Prince of Peace" (Isaiah 9:6).

During his life, Jesus made sure that God's promise was kept. He proved that he deserved all the wonderful names he received.

q

is for Quake

Remember those shepherds we talked about a while ago? Well, at first they weren't too thrilled when an angel and his friends appeared to them. The shepherds quaked—shook with terror—as light flashed across the night sky and heavenly beings stood before them. It must have been like meeting aliens from another planet!

But after hearing the angels sing—then hurrying off to see the baby Jesus—the shepherds felt much better. The Bible says that they returned to their flocks, praising God and celebrating the birth of Jesus (Luke 2:20).

r

is for Remember

It's easy to get the wrong idea about Christmas. Whether you're at the mall or just watching TV or surfing the Web, you see lots of stuff about Santa Claus, elves, reindeer, big sales, and new toys.

That's why it's important to remember the real hero of Christmas. If Christ hadn't been born in Bethlehem more than 2,000 years ago, we wouldn't be celebrating now. Let's not ever forget the person who gives Christmas its name.

S

is for Song

After learning that she would give birth to God's son, Mary was so happy that she composed a song (Luke 1:46-55). It begins, "My soul glorifies the Lord and my spirit rejoices in God my Savior, for he has been mindful of the humble state of his servant. From now on all generations will call me blessed, for the Mighty One has done great things for me—holy is his name."

This season, as you sing Christmas songs about our Lord, sing them with all your heart, the way Mary did.

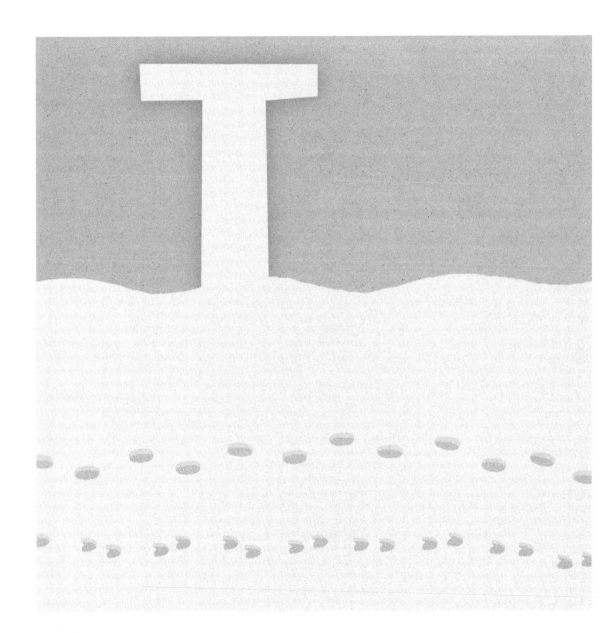

t

is for Three-Day Journey

In the days before Jesus was born, all the people in the Roman world were told to return to the town of their ancestors and sign their names to a huge list. The great emperor Caesar Augustus wanted to know exactly how many people he ruled over so that he could make them pay taxes (Luke 2:1–3).

So, Mary and Joseph had to travel for three long days from their home in Nazareth to Bethlehem. Imagine Joseph, walking for miles and miles, with Mary riding beside him on a donkey. Mary is nine months pregnant, and the long, dusty, bumpy ride makes her whole body ache. At last, the exhausted couple arrives at Bethlehem. They are so weary that sleeping in a smelly stable actually sounds pretty good.

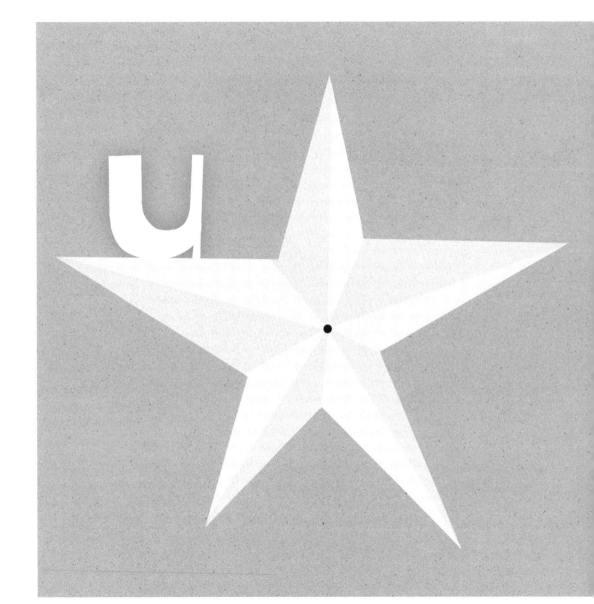

u

is for Unique

Jesus' birth is a unique event in human history. Christmas marks the first time that God came to earth in human form. Can you picture Jesus' tiny hands—hands that had carved out mountain ranges and formed the oceans—clinging to Mary's finger? Can you imagine the ruler of the Universe crying in hunger or shivering from the cold?

Jesus could have come to earth as a full-grown, powerful man. He could have been like a superhero. But he chose a harder, more humble beginning—not the kind of choice you'd expect from a king. That's why Christmas (and Christ) is unique.

V

is for Victory

Jesus' birth was a great victory for all of us. By coming to earth and becoming one of us, Jesus showed us how to live a sinless life. He showed us how to beat the temptation to do wrong things. Later, when he died for our sins, he made a way for us to live in heaven with him forever. All we have to do is trust in him.

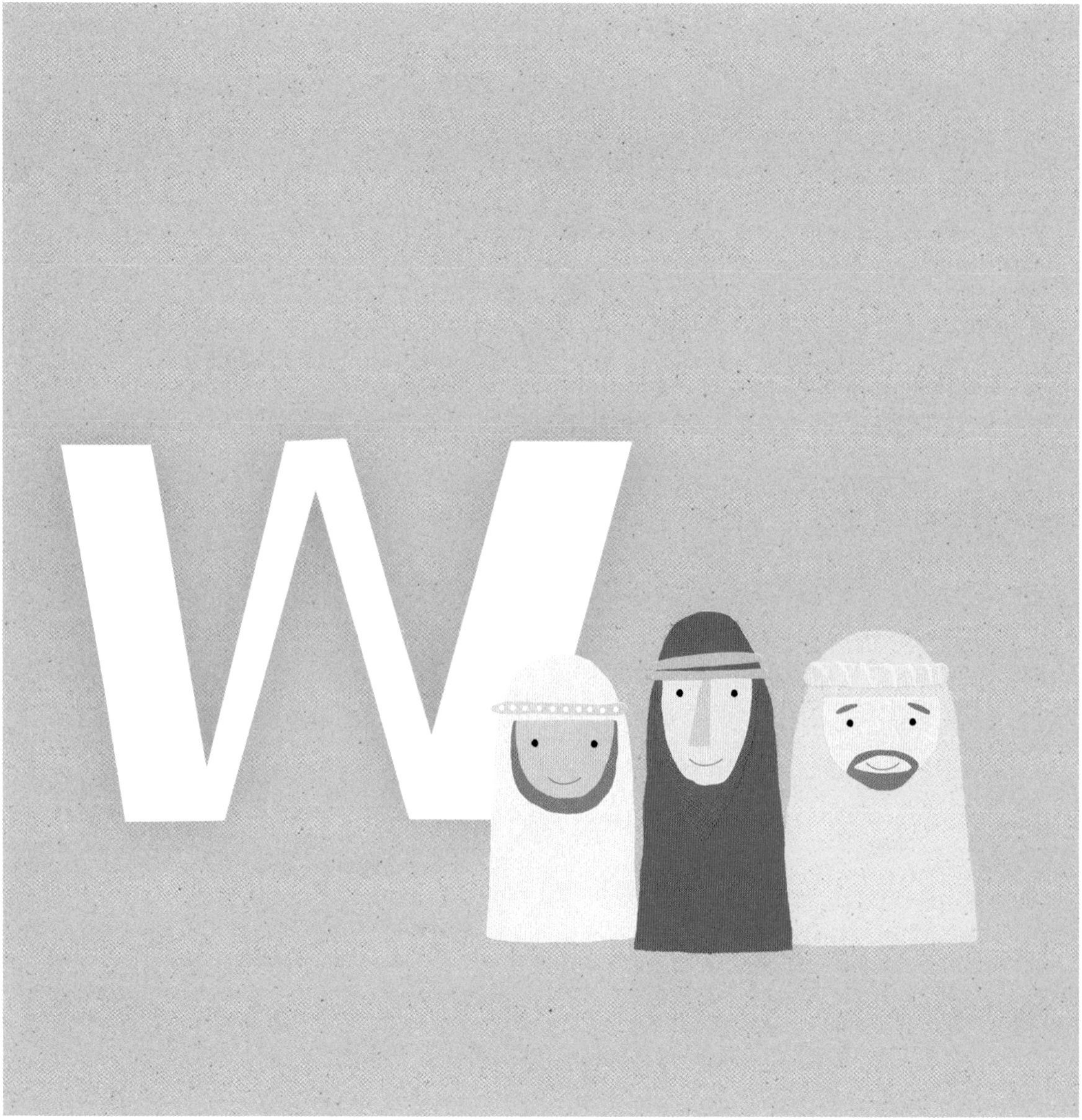
W

W
is for Wise Men

When Jesus was born, a shiny star appeared in the sky. Far away, some wise men who studied the stars saw this signal and left their homes to find Jesus. They had read that a special star would appear to signal the birth of a great king. So they followed the star, and it led them to the house where Jesus was staying after he was born (Matthew 2:9–11).

Imagine the wise men's wonder when they found the baby king. They knew this was no ordinary baby, so they bowed down and worshipped him. And they gave him the famous gifts of gold, frankincense, and myrrh.

By the way, we hear a lot about the three wise men, but the Bible doesn't say how many wise men visited Jesus. There were at least two, but there could have been five, ten, or even more! What do you think?

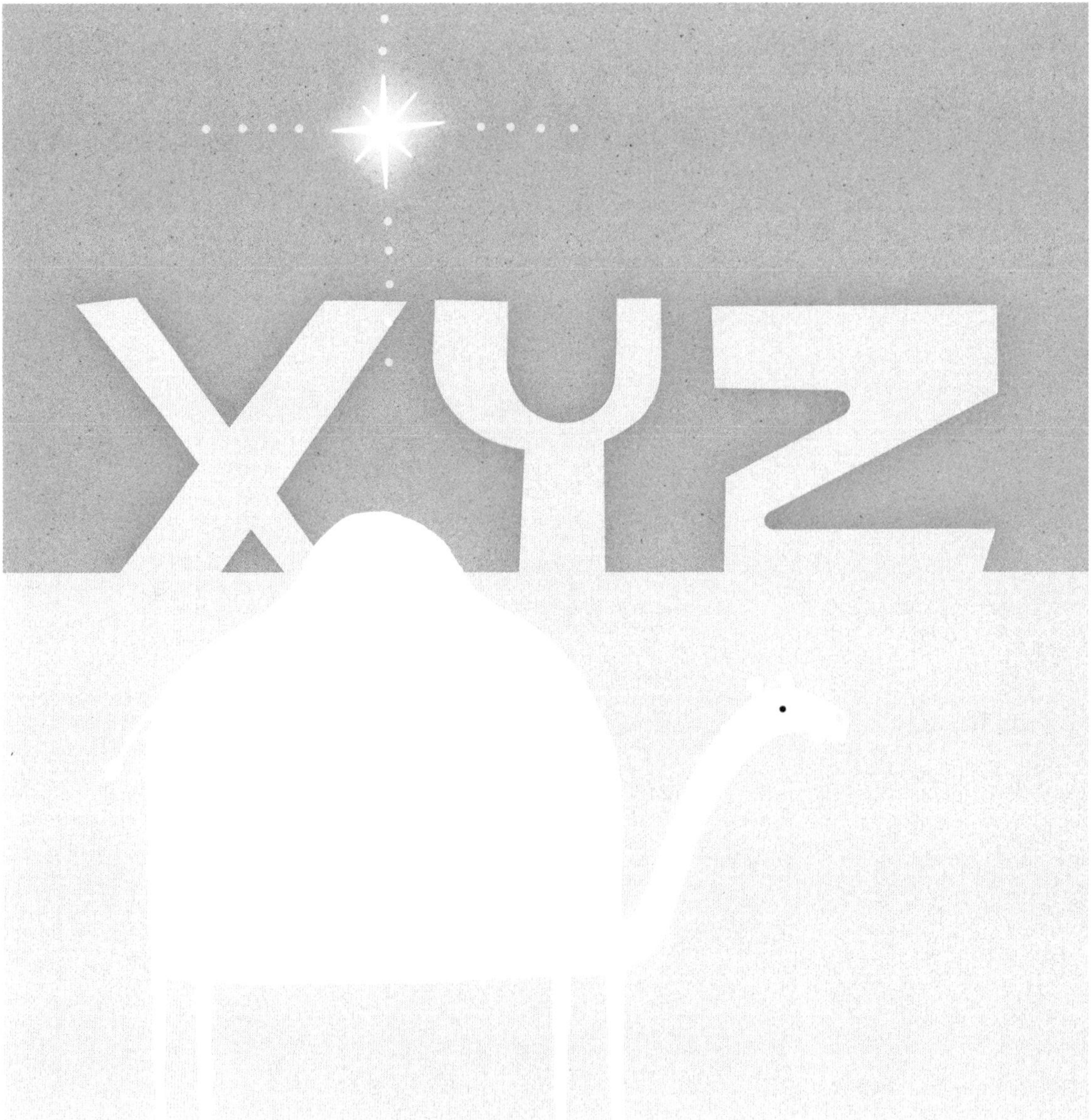
XYZ

xyz

the End

XYZ marks the end of the alphabet, and we've now arrived at the end of our Christmas journey. Of course, the letters X, Y, and Z all have a connection to Christmas, just like the rest of the alphabet:

Early Christians used X as a symbol for Christ. That's why you sometimes see Xmas used as a shorter way of writing Christmas.

Y is the first letter in Yahweh (Yah-way), the Hebrew word for God. When people like Abraham, David, and Moses prayed to God, they called him Yahweh.

As for the letter Z, Jesus referred to himself as "the A and the Z," the beginning and the ending (Revelation 1:8). This means that Jesus was present when the world was formed and that he'll rule over everything forever!

Congratulations!

Congratulations on reaching the end of your Christmas journey. Have a merry Christmas as you celebrate Jesus' birthday. And always remember that Christmas is a time for sharing the special love first demonstrated by God more than 2,000 years ago in the little town of Bethlehem.

We'd love to hear from you
if you have enjoyed this book.

PLEASE SEND YOUR COMMENTS TO:
Book Feedback, Mail Drop 215
2501 McGee, Kansas City, MO 64108
or e-mail us at
booknotes@Hallmark.com